Cel And Microbes

G000146433

Louise & Richard Spilsbury

Contents

OXFORD
UNIVERSITY PRESS

OXFORD

UNIVERSITY PRESS

Great Clarendon Street, Oxford OX2 6DP

Oxford University Press is a department of the University of Oxford. It furthers the University's objective of excellence in research, scholarship, and education by publishing worldwide in

Oxford New York

Auckland Cape Town Dar es Salaam Hong Kong Karachi Kuala Lumpur Madrid Melbourne Mexico City Nairobi New Delhi Shanghai Taipei Toronto

With offices in

Argentina Austria Brazil Chile Czech Republic France Greece Guatemala Hungary Italy Japan Poland Portugal Singapore South Korea Switzerland Thailand Turkey Ukraine Vietnam

OXFORD and OXFORD ENGLISH are registered trade marks of Oxford University Press in the UK and in certain other countries

© Oxford University Press 2010

The moral rights of the author have been asserted

Database right Oxford University Press (maker)

First published 2010
2017
10 9 8 7

No unauthorized photocopying

ISBN: 978 0 19 464563 8

An Audio Pack containing this book and an Audio download is also available, ISBN 978 0 19 402239 2

This book is also available as an e-Book, ISBN 978 0 19 464736 6

An accompanying Activity Book is also available, ISBN 978 0 19 464573 7

Printed in China

This book is printed on paper from certified and well-managed sources.

ACKNOWLEDGEMENTS

Illustrations by: Kelly Kennedy pp.4, 11, 14, 17, 23, 34; Ian Moores pp.11, 12, 15, 23, 40; Alan Rowe pp.36, 42, 50.

The Publishers would also like to thank the following for their kind permission to reproduce photographs and other copyright material: Alamy pp.3 and 5 (Biodisc/Visuals Unlimited/amoeba), 12 (Custom Life Science Images), 19 (Neil Hardwick), 35 (G&M Garden Images); Corbis pp.4 (Dennis Kunkel Microscopy, Inc./Visuals Unlimited), 10 (Jens Nieth/Corbis Edge/veins), 16 (Visuals Unlimited), 27 (Heide Benser/Solus/family), 30 (William Radcliffe/Science Faction), 33 (Jeon Heon-Kyun/epa); Getty Images p.21 (Mike Powell/Getty Images Sport), 31 (Chung Sung-Jun/Getty News Images); Oxford University Press p.6, 7 (plant/elephant), 9, 24, 27 (twins), 32; Photolibrary pp.3 (Dennis Kunkel/Phototake Science/blood cells), 8 (Garry DeLong/Oxford Scientific), 10 (Dennis Kunkel/Phototake Science/blood cells), 13 (Patti Murray/Animals Animals), 18 (BSIP – Phototake Science), 29 (C James Webb/Phototake Science), 38 (Garry DeLong/Oxford Scientific); Practical Action Images p.34 (Steven Hunt); Science Photo Library pp.17 (Manfred Kage), 20 (Thomas Deerinck, NCMIR), 22 (Dr Jeremy Burgess), 25 (Eye of Science), 26 (Christian Darkin), 28.

With thanks to Ann Fullick for science checking

Introduction

What are the smallest living things on Earth? The answer is cells. Some of the biggest living things, like whales, people, or trees, are made of millions of tiny cells! Microbes are living things that usually have just one cell.

How do we know about cells?
What types of cell do you know?
How many cells are there in your body?

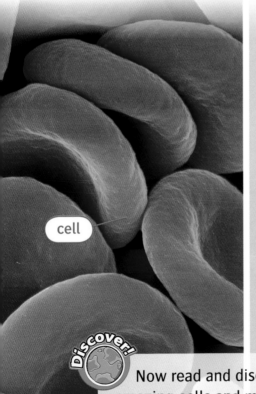

cell

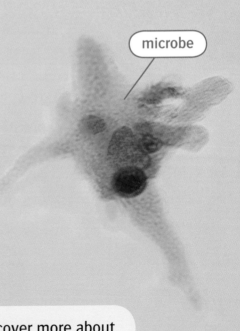

microbe

Discover!

Now read and discover more about amazing cells and microbes!

1 Discovering Cells

Most cells are too small to see, so how do people know that living things are made of cells? No one knew about cells until microscopes were invented. Microscopes magnify tiny things, like cells, to make them look bigger, so that people can see them.

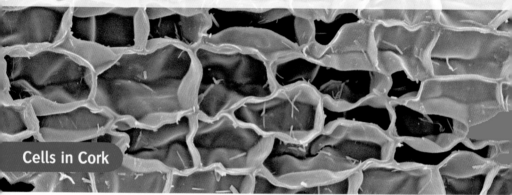

Cells in Cork

Learning About Cells

In 1665 a British scientist called Robert Hooke made one of the first microscopes. He used it to look at a thin piece of tree bark called cork. He saw that the cork was made of lots of tiny pieces. These were the cork cells. Today, microscopes can magnify things a million times!

Discover!

When Robert Hooke saw the pieces inside the cork, he called them 'cells' because they looked like little rooms called cells.

Living Cells

If cells are so small, how do we know if they are living or not? We know a cell is living because it does what other living things do. A cell can get energy from its food and a cell can move. A cell can grow so it can get bigger. A cell can reproduce – it can make more cells.

Most living things are made of many cells. The simplest living things are made of just one cell. We call them microbes because we can only see them through a microscope. An amoeba is one of the biggest types of microbe, but it's so small that 50 amoebas together are only as big as one grain of rice!

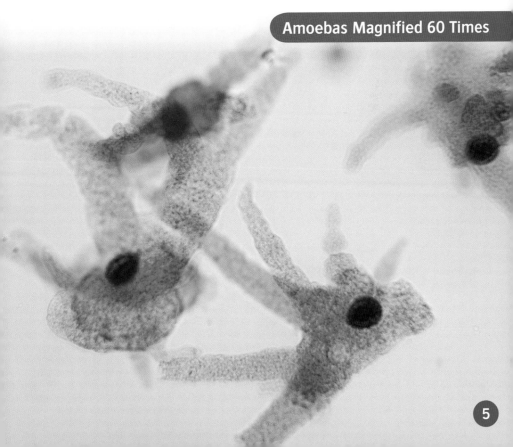

Amoebas Magnified 60 Times

Many Cells

Did you know that you started life as one cell? People, other animals, and plants grow from one cell into living things made of many cells. Different plants and animals are different sizes because of the number of cells in their body. An elephant is bigger than a rabbit because it has millions more cells.

Types of Cell

Not all cells are the same. Both plants and animals have different types of cell. For example, in plants some cells make food and other cells take in water.

The same cells that work together to do the same job are called tissues. For example, bark cells work together to make bark tissue on a tree. Skin cells make the skin tissue on an animal's body. Muscle cells make muscle tissues that help an animal to move.

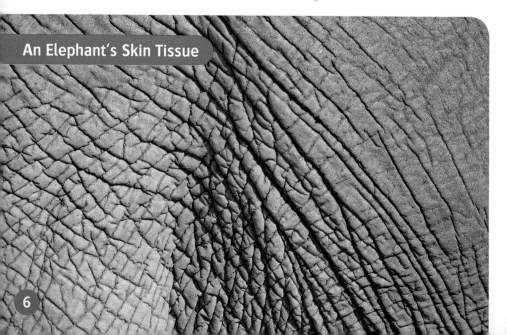

An Elephant's Skin Tissue

Some different tissues work together to make organs. Organs are important parts of the body, and they do amazing jobs. Eyes are organs that animals see with. Roots are organs that help plants to grow in soil.

An elephant's trunk is an important organ. The elephant uses it to pull leaves from trees and to lift other plant foods and water to its mouth. The trunk is made of different tissues, like skin tissue and muscle tissue.

soil

roots

An Elephant Using Its Trunk to Feed

→ Go to pages 36–37 for activities.

2 Animal Cells

The cells in an animal's body are different shapes and sizes, but they have the same important parts inside. Do you know what's inside an animal cell?

Inside Animal Cells

Animal cells have a cell membrane and a cytoplasm, and most cells also have a nucleus. The cell membrane is like a skin around the cytoplasm – it holds the cell together. It lets water and some other substances move through it to get in or out of the cell. It also stops other substances moving in or out.

Many important chemical reactions happen inside the cytoplasm. In some of these reactions, chemicals join together to make new substances for the cell to use. In other reactions, substances break down into smaller chemicals.

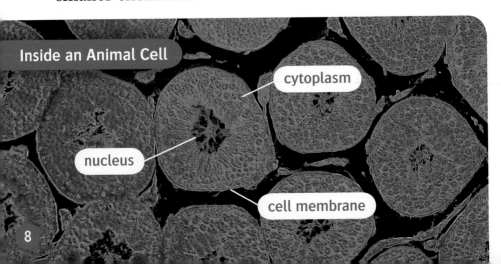

Inside an Animal Cell

cytoplasm

nucleus

cell membrane

The Cell Nucleus

The nucleus controls what happens inside the cell. Inside the nucleus there's a chemical code called DNA. The nucleus in every cell of an animal's body has the same code. This code controls how the cell grows, moves, and reproduces. It controls all the chemical reactions in the cell and the jobs that the cell does in the animal's body.

The DNA code in the nucleus also controls what an animal looks like. DNA codes make one type of animal look different from another animal. For example, it creates the different types of fish that we see in the oceans. DNA codes also make all the people in the world look different from each other.

Different Types of Fish with Different DNA

Red Blood Cells

People and other animals have different types of cell to do different jobs. Cells are different shapes and sizes, and this helps them to do their different jobs.

Red blood cells have a very important job to do. They take oxygen from the air to all the other cells in an animal's body. Animals need oxygen to live. Blood cells travel around an animal's body through blood vessels. Red blood cells are small, round, and flat. They look like tiny, soft cookies. Their shape helps them to move through thin blood vessels.

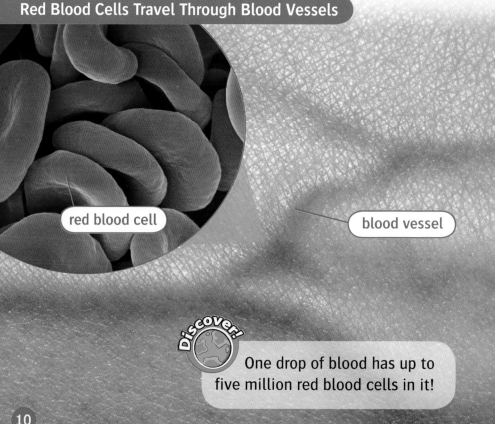

Red Blood Cells Travel Through Blood Vessels

red blood cell

blood vessel

Discover!

One drop of blood has up to five million red blood cells in it!

How Nerve Cells Work

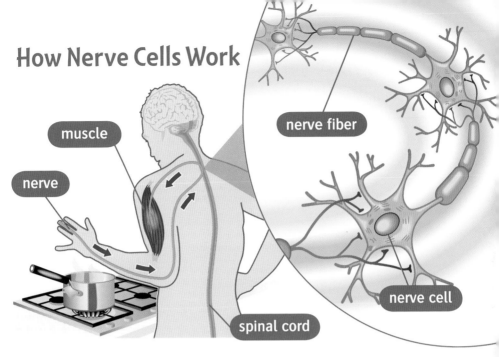

muscle

nerve fiber

nerve

spinal cord

nerve cell

There are nerve cells all around an animal's body. Nerve cells have long fibers to help nerves to send messages to each other.

Do you know how your nerve cells work when you touch something that's too hot? First, nerves in your hand send a message up your arm to your spinal cord. Nerves in your spinal cord send a message to the muscles in your arm, telling them to move your hand away from the heat. These messages are very fast and they are called reflexes. They help your body to stay safe.

Discover!

The nerve cells in a giraffe's neck are the longest cells in the world. One of these cells can be 3 meters long!

→ Go to pages 38–39 for activities.

3 Plant Cells

Like animal cells, plant cells have a cell membrane, a cytoplasm, and a nucleus. Plant cells also have other parts – a cell wall, a vacuole, and chloroplasts.

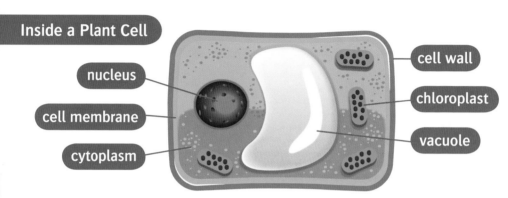

Inside a Plant Cell

nucleus

cell membrane

cytoplasm

cell wall

chloroplast

vacuole

The Cell Wall

Around the outside of the cell membrane of every plant cell there's a cell wall. This is like a box around the cell. The cell wall is made of cellulose fibers. Cellulose fibers are very strong and they help to give plant cells their shape. The strongest plant cell walls are in wood from trees.

Discover!

Some paper is made from cellulose. People put plant parts in water with special chemicals, and then they heat them to get the cellulose fibers out. Then they press the fibers together to make paper.

What Is a Vacuole?

The vacuole inside every plant cell is like a bag filled with water. The water gives the vacuole its shape and it helps to give the plant cell its shape. Many plant cells inside a plant are like lots of tiny bags of water. Together they press hard on the cell walls and help the plant to stand up. They make the plant stem stand up straight and they hold the leaves up into the light.

On a hot day, water dries up so there's less water for plants. When plant cells have less water, they do not stay the same shape. The plant cannot stand up any more and it wilts. Trees do not wilt because they have strong wood and bark to help them to stand up.

Plants Wilting on a Hot Day

How Chloroplasts Work

The chloroplasts in plant cells are very important. They give plant leaves and stems their green color, and they help the plant to make food. Like other living things, plants need food to live and grow.

When the sun shines on a leaf, chloroplasts inside leaf cells catch and store energy from the sunlight. The plant cells use this energy to help them to make sugar. Sugar is a type of food for the plant. Before plant cells can make sugar, they have to collect water and carbon dioxide. Water comes from the soil. It travels up the roots and into the leaves of the plant through little tubes inside the plant's stem. Carbon dioxide is a gas that comes from the air. The leaf takes in carbon dioxide through tiny holes called stomata.

When chloroplasts use the energy from sunlight to make sugar from carbon dioxide and water, it's called photosynthesis. The sugar moves from the leaves and through the stem to parts of the plant that need food.

During photosynthesis, plant cells also make oxygen. Plants let oxygen out of their leaves through their stomata so that it goes into the air. People and other animals use this oxygen to live.

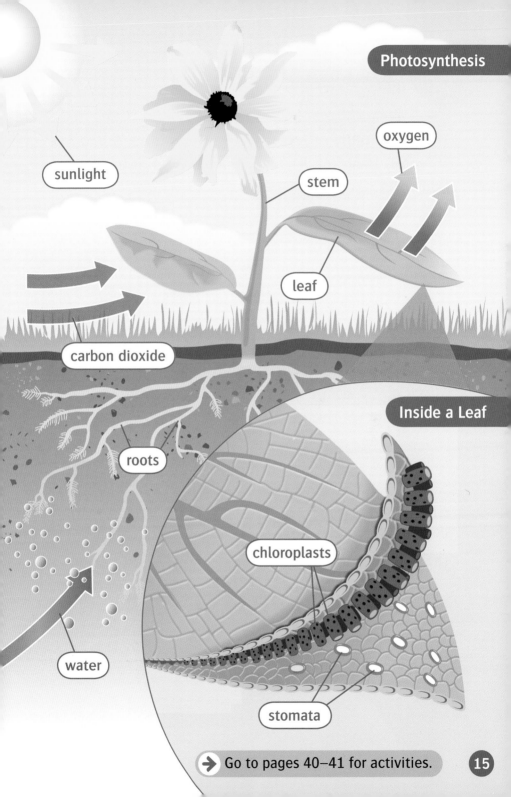

sunlight

oxygen

stem

leaf

carbon dioxide

Inside a Leaf

roots

chloroplasts

water

stomata

Go to pages 40–41 for activities.

4 Microbes

There are many different types of microbe. Some live in water, in air, or in soil. Others live on or inside the body of other living things.

Amoebas

An amoeba lives in wet places like ponds or soil, and it's so tiny that it's smaller than a grain of salt. An amoeba can make its body any shape. To feed, it moves around to find microbes that are smaller than it is. It catches these tiny microbes by making its body into a circle shape around them. Then the amoeba slowly digests them.

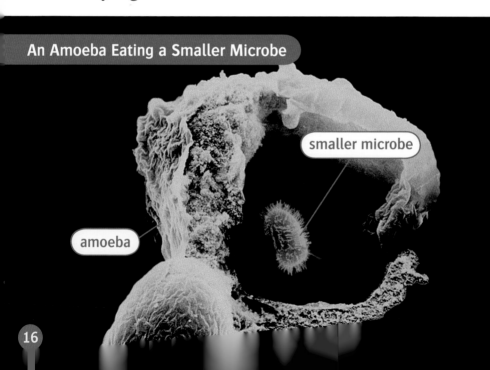

An Amoeba Eating a Smaller Microbe

smaller microbe

amoeba

Diatoms

Diatoms are microbes that live in water. Many live near the surface of the ocean. Like plant cells, diatoms have chloroplasts and they can use sunlight to make their own food by photosynthesis. The diatom's cell wall is different from the cell walls inside a plant. It's made of a substance that looks like thin glass. Different types of diatom are different shapes, and some look beautiful through a microscope.

Discover!

During photosynthesis, diatoms and other ocean microbes make half of all the oxygen in the air. So these tiny living things are very important for all of us!

17

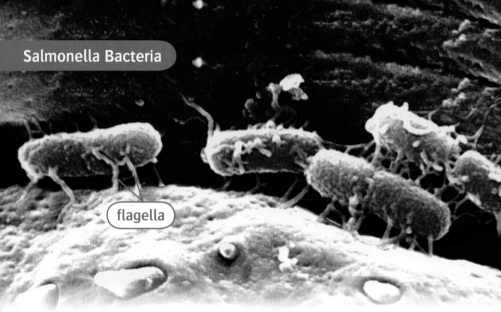

Salmonella Bacteria

flagella

Bacteria

Billions of years ago, bacteria were some of the first living things on Earth. Bacteria are microbes that live everywhere and there are many different types. Some bacteria make us sick, and some are very useful. Bacteria can eat almost anything. Some feed on waste, some eat oil, and some eat the food between people's teeth!

Bacteria are many different shapes. Some are like rods, some are like balls, and some are curly. Some have flagella that look like tiny hairs. These move in different directions to help the bacteria to move around.

Discover!

Some bacteria live in places like glaciers, high mountains, and volcanoes, where most other living things can't survive!

Slime Molds

Slime molds are types of microbe that usually live in gardens, on moldy leaves in woodlands, on wet soil, or on old trees. Like other microbes, every slime mold cell is tiny, but many slime mold cells join together into a group that travels to find food. This group of cells looks like a flat, messy pancake that can be yellow, orange, brown, or white. It moves very slowly across wood or soil to find bacteria, old leaves, or wood to eat. Then, like amoebas, the slime mold cells make themselves into a circle around their food before they eat it.

A Slime Mold

Go to pages 42–43 for activities.

5 How Cells Work

Plants, animals, and microbes need energy to stay alive. The cells of all living things take this energy from food.

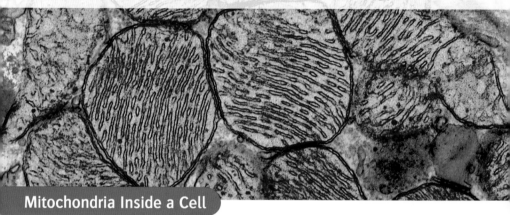

Mitochondria Inside a Cell

Making Energy

Mitochondria are tiny parts inside the cytoplasm of all cells, and they take energy from food. Cells that use a lot of energy, like the cells in muscle tissue and nerve tissue, have a lot of mitochondria. Inside the mitochondria, chemical reactions happen between oxygen and sugar. These reactions release energy from food. When living things use oxygen to release energy from food, it's called respiration.

Discover!

There's only very little oxygen in water at the bottom of the ocean. Microbes that live here can get energy from their food without oxygen.

20

Using Oxygen

Plant and animal cells use oxygen from the air for respiration. Plants take in oxygen for respiration through the stomata holes on their leaves. People and other animals take in oxygen by breathing it in through their mouth or nose.

When animals move very fast, like when people run in a race or play a fast game of soccer, their muscle cells use a lot of energy. These cells need more energy from food so that they can keep working. So animals start to breathe faster to take in more oxygen for respiration.

Runners Breathing Fast in a Race

In and Out

The cell membrane controls what goes in and out of every cell. It lets oxygen and sugar come into the cell for respiration. All chemical reactions make waste. During respiration, cells make waste carbon dioxide. The cell membrane lets carbon dioxide and other waste leave the cell.

Plant Root Cells

Plant roots have a type of cell called a root hair cell. These cells are very long. They grow from the root into the soil. The cell membranes on root hair cells are very thin so that water can go through them easily. Root hair cells collect most of the water that the plant needs and uses.

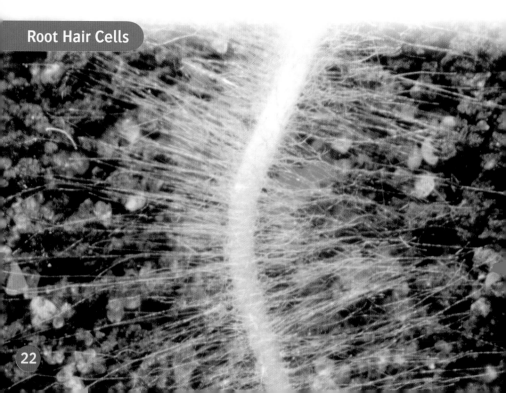

Root Hair Cells

How Diffusion Works

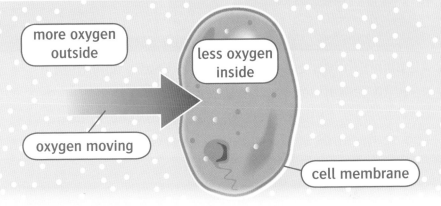

more oxygen outside

less oxygen inside

oxygen moving

cell membrane

The cell membrane has little holes that let in substances that are useful to the cell. Most substances move into a cell by diffusion. This is when a substance moves from where there's more of that substance to another place where there's less of it.

When there's more oxygen in an animal's blood than in its other cells, the oxygen moves from the blood into other cells. When there's more waste carbon dioxide inside a cell than outside it, the carbon dioxide moves out of the cell. Then it goes into the lungs and animals breathe it out.

Discover!

The cell membrane works like the doors that only let people in to a sports match if they have a ticket! It lets in substances that are useful to the cell.

➜ Go to pages 44–45 for activities.

All living things grow old and die. That's why they need to reproduce to create more living things like themselves. Cells divide to grow, to repair something, and sometimes to reproduce.

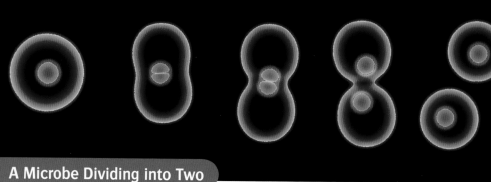

A Microbe Dividing into Two

Dividing into Two

Microbes, like amoebas and bacteria, reproduce by dividing into two. An amoeba breaks in half to create two new, smaller amoebas. These two new amoebas feed and grow and then they are ready to divide in half and make more new amoebas. All the new amoebas are the same as the first one.

Discover!

Bacteria reproduce very quickly. One cell can divide every 20 minutes and become five billion cells in just 11 hours!

Making New Cells

The cells that make the tissues and organs of plants and animals divide, too. They divide in half to create new cells that are the same as themselves, so that plants and animals can grow and get bigger. This is how the skin and muscles on a baby become bigger as the baby grows. This is also how plants become taller or grow new leaves. Plant and animal cells also make new cells to replace the ones that have become old or that have died. For example, skin cells divide to create new skin tissue to repair breaks in the skin when animals cut or hurt themselves.

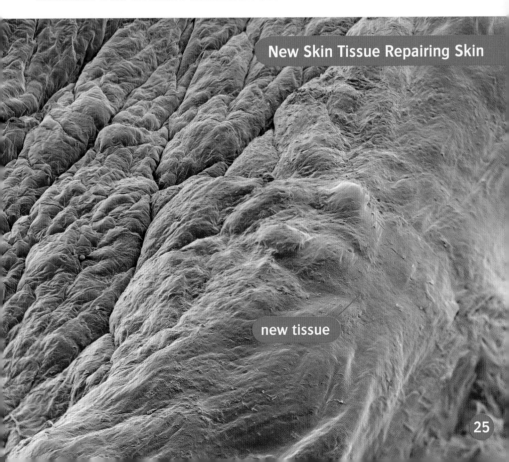

New Skin Tissue Repairing Skin

new tissue

Sex Cells

Microbes reproduce by dividing and creating other microbes that are the same as them. Most plants and animals reproduce differently from microbes. When people have a baby, the baby is not the same as its parents. This is because most plants and animals reproduce using sex cells.

With people, a man makes sex cells called sperm, and a woman makes sex cells called eggs. When a sperm and an egg join together, they create a new cell. This new cell divides again and again to make many cells. These cells become different types of cell, like skin and muscle cells, to make different parts of a baby.

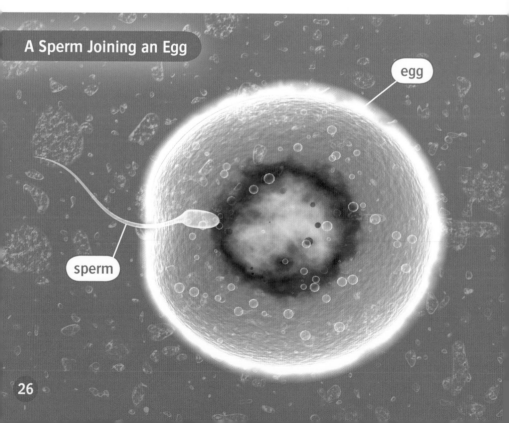

A Sperm Joining an Egg

egg

sperm

Each sex cell has only half the amount of DNA that other cells have. When the two sex cells join, the new cell has a complete set of DNA. The new cell nucleus has DNA codes from both parents – half from the mother and half from the father. That's why a baby grows up into an adult who looks a little like both parents, but is also different from both of them.

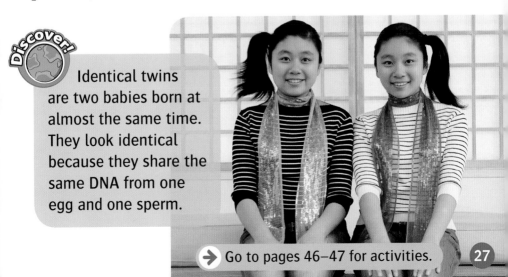

Discover!

Identical twins are two babies born at almost the same time. They look identical because they share the same DNA from one egg and one sperm.

→ Go to pages 46–47 for activities.

27

Cells and Infections

An infection is when microbes, like bacteria or viruses, make part of an animal's body sick. This is what happens when an ear infection gives you earache. Microbes reproduce quickly, so infections can make people and other animals sick very quickly, too.

Hunting Bacteria

White blood cells are very important because they can kill bacteria. Bacteria travel into a person's body on the food that they eat, in the air that they breathe in, or through their broken skin. White blood cells can move out of the blood to hunt, catch, and eat bacteria in other tissues. Some white blood cells create substances that make the bacteria weaker, so that it's easier for the other white blood cells to find and eat them.

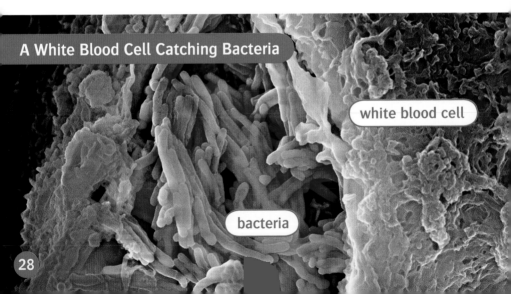

A White Blood Cell Catching Bacteria

white blood cell

bacteria

Antibiotics

Antibiotics are drugs that doctors give you to make you well when you are sick. Antibiotics only make you well if bacteria gave you the infection, like a throat infection that makes throats red and sore. Antibiotics work by killing bacteria or by stopping bacteria reproducing.

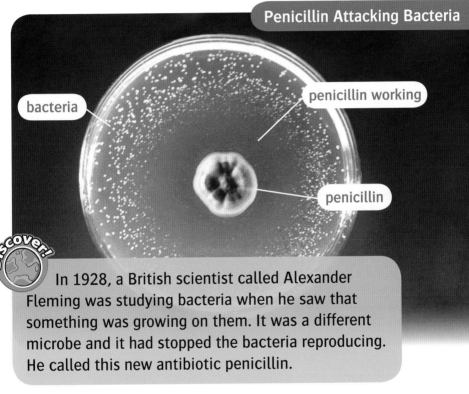

Penicillin Attacking Bacteria

bacteria

penicillin working

penicillin

Discover!

In 1928, a British scientist called Alexander Fleming was studying bacteria when he saw that something was growing on them. It was a different microbe and it had stopped the bacteria reproducing. He called this new antibiotic penicillin.

Why Is Washing Important?

Dirt on your fingers has bacteria in it. When you touch your mouth, the bacteria get inside you and they can make you sick. A simple way to stop this is to wash your hands before you eat food.

How Viruses Work

Viruses are another type of microbe that can make plants and animals sick. Viruses give people diseases like colds. They are much smaller than bacteria.

Most viruses travel into an animal's body in the air that it breathes in. In the body, the virus moves inside a cell and starts to grow there. It makes more and more viruses and then the cell breaks open. The other viruses get into more cells and make more viruses. Viruses move from person to person. If you have a cold and you sneeze, the viruses travel in the air and other people breathe them in.

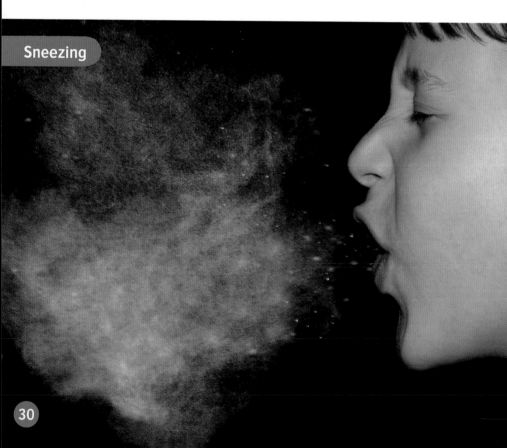

Sneezing

Finding Viruses

Antibiotics cannot kill viruses, but white blood cells can kill them when they break out of a cell. White blood cells know that viruses are invaders because viruses have chemicals that are not usually inside the body. After a virus has been inside a body, the white blood cells remember it. The next time this virus gets inside the body, they can find it and kill it more quickly.

Vaccinations

A vaccination is when doctors inject people with a small amount of a virus that would usually give them a serious infection. The virus is too weak to make people sick, but when it has been inside the body the white blood cells remember it, so they are ready to kill it in the future.

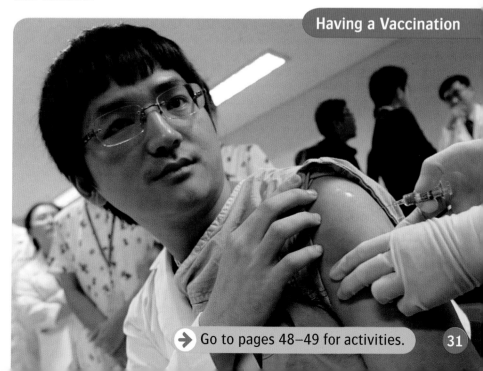

Having a Vaccination

Go to pages 48–49 for activities.

⑧ Useful Microbes

Do you know that there can be a kilogram of bacteria in a person's stomach? Don't be scared! Many microbes are very useful — they help people and Earth to stay well.

Foods That Help Your Stomach

Microbes Inside Us

After you eat, some of the bacteria in your stomach help your body to break down the food into sugar that your cells can use for energy. They also help you to get important substances like vitamins from the food, and they stop infections from bad bacteria, that can give you stomach ache. To help the useful bacteria in your stomach, you should eat more foods like fruit, vegetables, brown bread, and brown pasta. You shouldn't eat too many sweet and fatty foods like ice cream, chocolate, or French fries.

Microbes and Food

People use some microbes to make food. Yeasts are microbes that people use to make bread. When yeast is mixed with flour, salt, sugar, and water, it feeds on the sugar and makes carbon dioxide and other substances. The carbon dioxide makes the bread become bigger and lighter. When the bread is cooked, the other substances help to flavor it.

Storing Food

Some bacteria make lactic acid that stops food going bad, so that we can store it for longer. People use lactic acid bacteria to make foods like soy sauce, sauerkraut, and *kimchi*. To make *kimchi*, salt is mixed with cabbage. Bacteria eat sugar from the cabbage and make lactic acid that stops the cabbage going bad. This gives *kimchi* its sour flavor.

Making *Kimchi*, South Korea

33

A Biodigester, Sri Lanka

Microbes and Fuel

A fuel is a substance that people use to make heat and to make machines work. People use bacteria to change waste into fuel! They put plant and animal waste inside a biodigester, where bacteria feed on it. When they feed, the bacteria make a fuel called methane. The biodigester stores the methane so that people can use it for cooking food and heating water.

Discover!

If ships crash on rocks and drop oil in the ocean and on beaches, people sometimes put bacteria on the oil. The bacteria eat the oil and help to save the ocean animals.

Soil Microbes

There are bacteria in soil that help to break down plant and animal waste into tiny pieces. When they do this, they give back some of the nutrients from the waste into the soil. Plants use these nutrients to help them to grow. People make compost by collecting food waste and plant waste together. Bacteria in the waste help to break it down into compost. Farmers and gardeners mix the compost with soil to help plants to grow well. So without microbes like bacteria, there would be no life on Earth!

Puting Waste In

Taking Compost Out

Go to pages 50–51 for activities.

① Discovering Cells

← Read pages 4–7.

1 Write the words.

> microbe   tissue   scientist   ~~microscope~~   cell   organ

1 <u>microscope</u>   2 _____   3 _____

4 _____   5 _____   6 _____

2 Complete the sentences.

> ~~smallest~~   cell   microscope   million   amoeba

1 Cells are the ___smallest___ living things.

2 Scientists use a _____ to see cells.

3 Microscopes can magnify things a _____ times.

4 A living thing that is made of one _____ is called a microbe.

5 An _____ is one of the biggest microbes.

3 Circle the correct words.

1 Muscle cells make muscle **tissues** / **organs** that help animals to move.

2 Bark cells make the **bark** / **leaf** tissue on a tree.

3 An **eye** / **root** is an example of an animal organ.

4 In plants, different tissues make different organs, like **roots** / **trunks**.

4 Match.

1 There are different types of cell in

2 Tissues are the same

3 Cells that work together

4 Different tissues that work together make

cells that work together.

plant and animal bodies.

an organ.

do the same job.

5 Answer the questions.

1 Why are cells called cells?

Because they look like little rooms called cells.

2 What can cells do?

_____

_____

3 Have you ever seen cells through a microscope?

_____

_____

② Animal Cells

← Read pages 8–11.

1 Write the words.   nucleus   cytoplasm   cell membrane

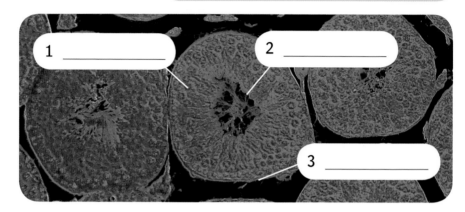

1 _____

2 _____

3 _____

2 Match.

1 The cell membrane

2 The nucleus controls

3 The cytoplasm

is where chemical reactions happen.

holds the cell together.

what happens inside the cell.

3 Circle the correct words.

1 Different cells do **different** / **the same** jobs in the body.

2 Red blood cells take **water** / **oxygen** to other cells.

3 Red blood cells are small, **round** / **square**, and flat.

4 Blood travels through blood **vessels** / **nerves**.

5 One drop of blood has up to **five** / **two** million red blood cells in it.

4 **Order the words.**

1 The / of the cell. / lets substances / move inside and out / cell membrane

   The cell membrane lets substances move inside
   and out of the cell.

2 for the cell. / in the cytoplasm / Some chemical reactions / make new substances

   _____

3 the nucleus / called DNA. / there's a chemical code / Inside

   _____

4 controls how / the cell grows, / moves, and reproduces. / DNA

   _____

5 **Answer the questions.**

1 Where do we find nerve cells?

   _____

2 What do nerve cells look like?

   _____

3 How do nerve cells send messages to each other?

   _____

4 How do reflexes help us?

   _____

③ Plant Cells

← Read pages 12–15.

1 Write the words.

nucleus   cytoplasm   cell membrane
cell wall   chloroplast   vacuole

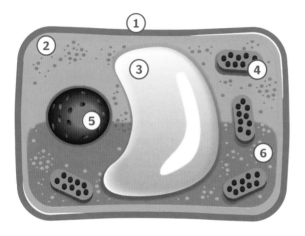

1 _____

2 _____

3 _____

4 _____

5 _____

6 _____

2 Write *true* or *false*.

1 Vacuoles are filled with fibers.   _false_

2 The water in vacuoles gives them their shape.   _____

3 Vacuoles press on cell walls to help a plant
   to stand up.   _____

4 Plants wilt when they have too much water.   _____

5 Trees do not wilt because they have strong
   wood and bark.   _____

3 Circle the correct words.

1 Like animal cells, plants cells have a cell membrane, a cytoplasm, and a **cellulose** / **nucleus**.

2 The cell wall is around the **outside** / **inside** of a plant cell.

3 The cell wall is made of **chloroplast** / **cellulose** fibers.

4 Cellulose fibers help to give plant cells their **shape** / **color**.

5 Cell walls in wood are the **weakest** / **strongest**.

6 People use cellulose fibers to make **sandwiches** / **paper**.

4 Match. Then write the sentences.

Chloroplasts give leaves and stems	and water to make food.
Chloroplasts catch and store	food for the plant.
Plants take in water	through holes called stomata.
Leaves take in carbon dioxide	through their roots.
Plant cells use carbon dioxide	energy from sunlight.
Sugar is a type of	their green color.

1 Chloroplasts give leaves and stems their green color.

2 _____

3 _____

4 _____

5 _____

6 _____

(4) Microbes

← Read pages 16–19.

1 Write the words. amoeba bacteria slime mold diatom

1 _____

2 _____

3 _____

4 _____

2 Correct the sentences.

1 There are a few different types of microbe.

   There are many different types of microbe.

2 Microbes live in a few different places.

   _____

3 An amoeba is bigger than a grain of salt.

   _____

4 Amoebas eat microbes that are bigger than they are.

   _____

5 An amoeba quickly digests its food.

   _____

3 Order the words.

1 looks like / The cell wall / of a diatom / thin glass.

_____

2 Bacteria were / on Earth. / some of the / first living things

_____

3 people's teeth. / eat the food / Some bacteria / between

_____

4 where / Some bacteria / can't. / other living things / survive

_____

4 Answer the questions.

1 How do amoebas catch their food?

_____

2 How do diatoms make their food?

_____

3 What do bacteria eat?

_____

4 How do slime molds travel to find food?

_____

5 Why are diatoms and other ocean microbes important for all of us?

_____

5 How Cells Work

← Read pages 20–23.

1 Find and write the words.

1 _mitochondria_

2 o _____

3 r _____

4 e _____

5 b _____

6 d _____

7 w _____

8 c _____

9 l _____

10 b _____

m	i	t	o	c	h	o	n	d	r	i	a
e	x	b	z	a	a	x	u	q	e	b	e
g	t	t	u	a	b	y	w	e	c	l	w
e	n	e	r	g	y	g	b	s	e	o	a
f	q	w	c	d	x	e	o	o	l	o	s
a	f	g	h	t	s	n	a	w	l	d	t
b	r	e	a	t	h	i	n	g	s	a	e
l	u	n	g	s	r	t	w	i	m	s	w
e	r	e	s	p	i	r	a	t	i	o	n
t	x	d	i	f	f	u	s	i	o	n	z

2 Circle the correct words.

1 Mitochondria are **inside** / **outside** the cytoplasm.

2 Mitochondria release energy from **food** / **air**.

3 Chemical reactions happen between **carbon dioxide** / **oxygen** and sugar.

4 Cells that use **little** / **a lot of** energy have a lot of mitochondria.

3 Order the words. Then answer the questions.

1 what goes in and out? / What part / controls / of a cell

   What part of a cell controls what goes in and out?
   The cell membrane controls what goes in and out.

2 chemical reactions / make? / What do all / in a cell

   _____

   _____

3 of waste / What type / do cells / during respiration? / make

   _____

   _____

4 do with waste? / What does / membrane / the cell

   _____

   _____

4 Complete the sentences.

more   diffusion   less   Oxygen   Carbon dioxide

1 Most substances move into a cell by _____ .

2 Diffusion is when a substance moves from where there's
   _____ of that substance to another place where
   there's _____ of it.

3 _____ moves from the blood into other cells by
   diffusion.

4 _____ moves out of a cell by diffusion.

6 Dividing and Reproducing

← Read pages 24–27.

1 Write *true* or *false*.

1 No living things grow old and die. _____

2 Living things reproduce to make more
living things like themselves. _____

3 Cells can divide to grow and repair themselves. _____

4 No cells divide to reproduce. _____

5 Bacteria reproduce very slowly. _____

6 One bacteria cell can become five billion
cells in just one hour. _____

2 Circle the correct words.

1 Microbes, like amoebas, reproduce by dividing into **two** / **four**.

2 An amoeba breaks in half to create two **smaller** / **bigger**
amoebas.

3 The new amoebas feed and **grow** / **get smaller**.

4 When amoebas grow, they are ready to **divide** / **die**.

5 New amoebas are **different from** / **the same as** the first
amoeba.

3 Complete the puzzle.

1 Plants and animals ___ using sex cells.

2 A woman's sex cells are called ___ .

3 ___ twins have the same DNA.

4 A man's sex cells are called ___ .

5 Each sex cell has half the amount of ___ .

6 When a sperm and an egg join they create a new ___ .

7 The new cell has a ___ set of DNA.

8 ___ may look like their parents because they share DNA.

1 ↓ r
e
p
r
o
d
u
c
e

2 → e
4 → r
5 → d
6 → c
7 →
8 →
3 ↓

4 Answer the questions.

1 How do plant and animal cells create new cells?

_____

2 When skin cells divide, what new cells do they create?

_____

3 Why do plant and animal cells create new cells?

_____

7 Cells and Infections

← Read pages 28–31.

1 Match.

1 An infection is when

2 Ear infections

3 Bacteria get into a body on

4 Some white blood cells

5 Some white blood cells

food, air, or broken skin.

give you earache.

hunt, catch, and eat bacteria.

bacteria or viruses make an animal sick.

make bacteria weak and easier to catch.

2 Order the words. Then answer the questions.

1 does dirt / have in it? / on your fingers / Which microbes

_____

_____

2 bacteria / How do / get / into your mouth?

_____

_____

3 get inside you? / do if they / What can / some bacteria

_____

_____

4 getting / bacteria in dirt / inside your body? / How can you stop

_____

_____

3 Write *true* or *false*.

1 Antibiotics are infections that doctors give you. _____

2 Antibiotics can stop infections created by viruses. _____

3 Antibiotics work by killing bacteria
or stopping bacteria reproducing. _____

4 Alexander Fleming discovered the
antibiotic penicillin. _____

4 Complete the sentences. Then write sentences with the extra words.

> sneezes Antibiotics invaders diseases
> microbes breathe chemicals vaccination

1 Viruses are _____ that can make plants and animals sick.

2 Viruses give people _____ like colds.

3 When someone who has a cold _____ , the viruses travel in the air.

4 People can take viruses into their body on the air that they _____ in.

5 _____ cannot kill viruses.

6 Viruses have _____ that are not usually inside the body.

7 _____

8 _____

8 Useful Microbes

← Read pages 32–35.

1 Complete the chart.

Foods that give us useful bacteria:
fruit

Foods that don't give us useful bacteria:

2 Answer the questions.

1 What do useful bacteria help your stomach to do?

_____

2 What do your cells use sugar for?

_____

3 How can you help the useful bacteria in your stomach?

_____

4 How do useful bacteria help to stop stomach ache?

_____

3 Circle the correct words.

1 Lactic acid stops food going **cold** / **bad.**

2 Bacteria eat **sugar** / **salt** in some foods and then they make lactic acid.

3 People use **lactic acid** / **lemon juice** to make soy sauce.

4 *Kimchi* is made from salt and **cabbage** / **cheese.**

4 Complete the sentences.

oil   waste   methane   fuel   biodigester   nutrients

1 A _____ is a substance that people use to make machines work.

2 Bacteria can change _____ into fuel.

3 Inside a _____ , bacteria feed on plant and animal waste to make fuel.

4 The biodigester makes a fuel called _____ .

5 People put bacteria on oil on beaches, and the bacteria eat the _____ .

6 Bacteria in soil help to give back _____ from waste into soil.

5 Write about microbes. Which microbes help us and which microbes can make us sick?

_____

_____

_____

A New Microbe

1 Imagine a new type of microbe. Write notes.

What shape and color is it?

_____

_____

Where does it live?

_____

_____

What does it eat?

_____

_____

How does it move?

_____

_____

How does it reproduce?

_____

_____

Does it hurt or help people?

_____

_____

2 Draw your microbe and write about it.

3 Display your work.

A Bacteria Poster

1 Write notes and complete the diagram about how washing your hands helps to stop bacteria making you sick.

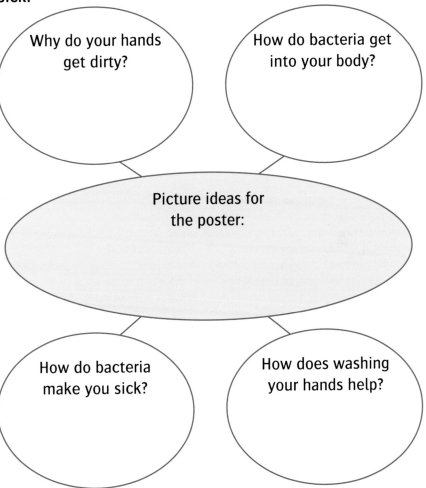

Why do your hands get dirty?

How do bacteria get into your body?

Picture ideas for the poster:

How do bacteria make you sick?

How does washing your hands help?

2 Make a poster using the information from your diagram. Write sentences and draw or add pictures.

3 Display your poster.

Glossary

adult a person or animal that has finished growing

alive living

antibiotic a drug that stops bacteria working

bark the brown, hard part around the body of a tree

blood the red liquid in your body

break down to become smaller and smaller pieces

breathe to take in and let out air through your nose and mouth

carbon dioxide a gas in the air

cell the smallest living thing

cellulose something that makes the walls of plant cells

change to become different; to make something different

chemical a solid or liquid that is made by chemistry

chemical reaction a change that creates a new substance from other materials

child (*plural* **children**) a very young person

complete when something has everything that it needs

compost food and plant waste that people can use to help plants grow

control to make someone or something else do something

die to stop living

digest you do this when you eat food

dirt something that is not clean

disease a medical problem that makes you sick

divide to break something into smaller parts

DNA the code in cells that makes living things what they are

drop a very small amount of liquid

drug a substance that doctors give you to make you well when you are sick

energy we need energy to move and grow, and machines need energy to work

fatty with lots of fat; fatty foods are foods like cream, butter, and ice cream

fiber something that looks like a thin string

fuel something that we use to produce heat or energy

gas not a solid or a liquid; like air

glass a hard material; you can make windows and bottles with it

grain the small, hard seed of a food plant like wheat or rice

group a number of people or things that are together

grow to get bigger

heat to make something hot

hole a space in something

hurt to give pain

identical the same as someone or something else

inject to put a drug into someone's arm or other part of the body

invader a living thing that goes where it's not wanted

kill to make something or someone die

lactic acid a substance that can stop food going bad

leaf (*plural* **leaves**) the flat, green part of a plant

liquid not a solid or a gas; like water

lung a part of the body that takes in and lets out air

magnify to make something look bigger

methane a type of gas

microbe (*also* **micro-organism**) a tiny living thing

microscope a machine that makes tiny things look bigger

muscle a part of your body that helps to move your bones

neck a part of an animal's body that holds up the head

nerve a type of cell that sends messages around an animal's body

nutrient something that we get from food to live and grow

oil a smooth, thick liquid

oxygen a gas that we need to breathe

photosynthesis the way that plants use sunlight to make sugar for food

reflex what an animal does when it moves without thinking about it

release to let something out or make it free

repair to put something that is broken back together again

replace to put a new thing back in the place of an old one

reproduce to make more living things like oneself

rod a long, straight stick

root the part of a plant that holds it in the soil

sauerkraut small pieces of cabbage with a sour flavor

sex cell a type of cell that living things use to reproduce

shape for example, circle, square, triangle

share to have or use something at the same time as someone else

ship a large boat

size how big or small someone or something is

soil the ground that plants grow in

sour having a taste like a lemon or a fruit that is not ready to eat

stem the part of a plant that holds it up

stomach a part of the body that helps to digest food

substance a type of material

sunlight light from the sun

surface the top part of something

survive to live

tiny very small

tissue the same cells that work together to do the same job

tube a long, round thing that has a tunnel going through it

useful that helps someone to do something

vaccination it stops a person or animal getting a disease

vegetable a plant or part of a plant that we eat as food

virus a tiny living thing that can make people sick

vitamin something in food that makes us healthy

waste things that we throw away

wilt when a plant falls down because it has too little water

without not having something; not doing something

woodland a place where many trees grow

Oxford Read and Discover

Series Editor: Hazel Geatches • CLIL Adviser: John Clegg

Oxford Read and Discover graded readers are at six levels, for students from age 6 and older. They cover many topics within three subject areas, and support English across the curriculum, or Content and Language Integrated Learning (CLIL).

Available for each reader:
• Audio Pack
• Activity Book

Available for selected readers:
• e-Books

Teaching notes & CLIL guidance: **www.oup.com/elt/teacher/readanddiscover**

Subject Area / Level	The World of Science & Technology	The Natural World	The World of Arts & Social Studies
1 300 headwords	• Eyes • Fruit • Trees • Wheels	• At the Beach • In the Sky • Wild Cats • Young Animals	• Art • Schools
2 450 headwords	• Electricity • Plastic • Sunny and Rainy • Your Body	• Camouflage • Earth • Farms • In the Mountains	• Cities • Jobs
3 600 headwords	• How We Make Products • Sound and Music • Super Structures • Your Five Senses	• Amazing Minibeasts • Animals in the Air • Life in Rainforests • Wonderful Water	• Festivals Around the World • Free Time Around the World
4 750 headwords	• All About Plants • How to Stay Healthy • Machines Then and Now • Why We Recycle	• All About Desert Life • All About Ocean Life • Animals at Night • Incredible Earth	• Animals in Art • Wonders of the Past
5 900 headwords	• Materials to Products • Medicine Then and Now • Transportation Then and Now • Wild Weather	• All About Islands • Animal Life Cycles • Exploring Our World • Great Migrations	• Homes Around the World • Our World in Art
6 1,050 headwords	• Cells and Microbes • Clothes Then and Now • Incredible Energy • Your Amazing Body	• All About Space • Caring for Our Planet • Earth Then and Now • Wonderful Ecosystems	• Food Around the World • Helping Around the World